D0932529

APOSTOLISCHE NUNTIATUR
IN DEUTSCHLAND

Dear Professor!

A short time ago I had the occasion to bring the Holy Father's attention to your booklet "The Encyclical *Humanae Vitae*: A Sign of Contradiction," which has just been published by Habbel, Regensburg, Germany.

The Pontifical Secretariat of State has now sent me the message from the Holy Father that His Holiness expressed the wish that his gratitude and his appreciation for this work be conveyed to you.

I am happy to perform this task for it affords me the opportunity to greet you after so many years. I am reading your book *The Trojan Horse* . . . Such works and such a position are very much needed in the Church today.

I obtained your address through your son whom I met at the burial of your nephew, the Ambassador to the Holy See, Sattler, whose death was most untimely and who was respected by everyone.

I would be most happy if you would give me the joy of paying me a visit when you again travel to Germany, and would be happy if you would accept the hospitality of the Apostolic Nunciature.

With kind greetings and best wishes.

Devotedly,

*Konrad Bafile*

Konrad Bafile
Apostolic Nuncio

Prof. Dr. Dietrich von Hildebrand
43 Calton Road
New Rochelle, N. Y. 10804

# THE ENCYCLICAL
# HUMANAE VITAE
## A Sign of Contradiction

# By Dietrich von Hildebrand

## In English

*In Defense of Purity*
*Marriage*
*Transformation in Christ*
*Christian Ethics*
*The New Tower of Babel*
*Graven Images: Substitutes for True Morality*
*Liturgy and Personality*
*What is Philosophy?*
*Not as the World Gives*
*The Sacred Heart*
*The Art of Living*
*Man and Woman*
*Morality and Situation Ethics*
*Trojan Horse in the City of God*

## In German

*Die Idee der sittlichen Handlung*
*Sittlichkeit und ethische Werterkenntnis*
*Metaphysik der Gemeinschaft*
*Das Katholische Berufsethos*
*Engelbert Dollfuss: Ein Katholischer Staatsmann*
*Der Sinn philosophischen Fragens und Erkennens*
*Die Menschheit am Scheideweg*
*Mozart, Beethoven und Schubert*

# THE ENCYCLICAL
# HUMANAE VITAE

## A Sign of Contradiction

*An Essay on Birth Control
and Catholic Conscience*

by

**DIETRICH VON HILDEBRAND**

FRANCISCAN HERALD PRESS
1434 WEST 51st STREET • CHICAGO, 60609

The American edition of *The Encyclical "Humanae Vitae"* — *A Sign of Contradiction* represents a translation and enlargement of the original German edition, *Die Enzyklika "Humanae Vitae" — ein Zeichen des Wiederspruchs.* Translated by Damian Fedoryka and John Crosby. Published by Habbel, Regensburg, 1968. Copyright 1969 by Franciscan Herald Press, 1434 West 51st Street, Chicago, Illinois 60609. Library of Congress Catalog Card Number: 71-78991. Designed by Publication Associates. Made in the United States of America.

●·0·●=0·●=0·●=0·●=0·●=0·●=0·●=0·●=0·●=0·●=0·●=0·●=0·●=0·●=0·●=0·●=0·●=0·●=0·●=0·●

NIHIL OBSTAT:
  Marion A. Habig O.F.M.
  *Censor Deputatus*

IMPRIMATUR:
  Rt. Rev. Msgr. Francis W. Byrne
  *Vicar General, Archdiocese of Chicago*


February 4, 1969

To my dear friend in Christ

WILLIAM FITZPATRICK

faithful fighter for truth

# CONTENTS

Introduction ................................................................xi

PART I: SEX, LOVE AND MARRIAGE ...................... 1
Chapter 1: Marriage as a community of love ................... 3
Chapter 2: Errors concerning marriage ........................... 5
Chapter 3: The value of sex as the expression and
               fulfillment of spousal love and the sin
               of isolating it ......................................... 9
Chapter 4: Marriage as *"remedium concupiscentiae"* ......11
Chapter 5: False reaction to the puritanical suspicion
               of marriage: idolization of sexual pleasure ....11
Chapter 6: Essential differences between true spousal
               love and isolated sexual desire .....................13
Chapter 7: Prudishness, neutral attitude or reverence
               and modesty? .............................................21
Chapter 8: Spousal love and the irrevocable union
               of marriage ..............................................22
Chapter 9: The supernatural transformation
               of marriage ..............................................24

PART II: MARRIAGE AND PROCREATION ...........27
Chapter 1: The meaning of marriage and the principle
               of superabundant finality ..........................29
Chapter 2: The meaning of marriage and its
               primary end ............................................34
Chapter 3: Why artificial birth control is sinful .............35
Chapter 4: Two concepts of nature in *Humanae Vitae*....38
Chapter 5: The relation between biological nature and
               the person ...............................................42
Chapter 6: Why artificial birth control is sinful but
               the rhythm method is not ...........................46

PART III: FURTHER OBJECTIONS TO THE
ENCYCLICAL *HUMANAE VITAE* ...........................51
Chapter 1: Is the Church's teaching on marriage and
               procreation impossible to live up to? ........53
Chapter 2: Inhibition of spontaneity ..........................54

PART IV: THE ENCYCLICAL *HUMANAE VITAE*
AND OUR ATTITUDE ........................................................57
Chapter 1: Does obedience presuppose infallibility? ......59
Chapter 2: Natural moral law and the magisterium ........60
Chapter 3: Sacrifice and the absolute primacy of
           the moral sphere .............................................61

PART V: CONSCIENCE AND THE
MAGISTERIUM ..................................................................63
Chapter 1: Conscience and the knowledge of the
           moral law .........................................................65
Chapter 2: Conscience and desire ...................................67
Chapter 3: Competence and the magisterium .................75
Chapter 4: The interpretation of the objective moral
           law by the magisterium of the Church and
           the duty of the individual conscience .........82

PART VI: THE ENCYCLICAL *HUMANAE VITAE*
AND THE CREDO OF PAUL VI ...................................85

# INTRODUCTION

The reaction of many to the encyclical *Humanae Vitae* indicates a widespread lack of understanding of the true nature of marriage.

For years I have defended the position that marriage, as well as the marital act, has meaning not only because of procreation, but also as the expression and fulfillment of a deep union of love. It was occasionally said that by affirming that the marital act retains a meaning and high value even when — through no intervention of ours — conception cannot occur, I was opening the door to a justification of artificial birth control. But this approach showed a misapprehension of my position, for I had emphatically stated in many articles and books that artificial birth control cannot be allowed. It was precisely my intention to call attention to the great mystery of God's having entrusted the generation of a new human being to the most intimate union of love. The dignity and beauty of the marital act as an irrevocable mutual self-donation in which the two spouses become "one flesh" cause the mysterious link between this act and the birth of a new human being to shine forth in all nobility and grandeur.

Today, a number of Catholics and priests still make this mistake: if the role of love in marriage is emphasized, they conclude that artificial birth control must be allowed. Because the Second Vatican

Council has stressed the marital act as the fulfillment of mutual love and irrevocable union, they decide that artificial birth control may be permitted
when there are important reasons for preventing
pregnancy. This old misunderstanding accounts for
the failure to see that from the moral point of view
there is an abyss separating the observance of rhythm
from artificial birth control.

Let us openly admit that this misapprehension
has been facilitated by the many erroneous arguments against artificial birth control which in the
past were set forth in books and from the pulpit
and which are still often invoked in defense of the
encyclical *Humanae Vitae.*

Among those who react negatively to the encyclical of the Holy Father, two groups must be clearly
distinguished.

The first group is composed primarily of faithful
married Catholics who, though uninfected by the
movement of secularization, are understandably very
disappointed; for despite Vatican II's declaration
to the contrary and despite the official teaching of
the Church in this matter,[1] many spiritual advisors
and confessors had been telling them that the use of

---

1. Cf. *Gaudium et Spes,* 51: "Relying on these prin-
ciples (based on the nature of the human person
and his acts), sons of the Church may not undertake methods of regulating procreation which are
found blameworthy by the teaching authority of
the Church in its unfolding of the divine law."
(At this point in the Council text there is a note
referring to *Casti Connubii* of Pius XI and to addresses of Pius XII and Paul VI.) Cf. "Amoralism," Chapter 21, *Trojan Horse in the City of God,*
rev. ed. (Chicago: Franciscan Herald Press, 1968).

the pill is morally unobjectionable should serious reasons for prevention of pregnancy arise. It is naturally difficult for them to renounce the pill as a solution to their problems, now that they have grown accustomed to considering it legitimate. (Far be it from us not to feel a deep sympathy for those married couples who are obliged by the uncertainty they experience in the rhythm method to observe more or less complete abstinence because conception would endanger the health and, possibly, the life of the wife.)

This first group also includes spiritual advisors who, despite their faith in the Church, taught out of compassion that the pill is allowed in these cases.

Nevertheless, it must be realized that we cannot tailor the will of God to human desires or permit a sin just because avoiding it entails great sacrifice. Therefore, for this group above all, a clear delineation of the conduct God wills, presented by the highest authority of the Church, is especially desirable. It is moreover important that they understand the true *reason* for the sinfulness of artificial birth control; for the more clearly a person perceives why a thing is sinful, the more easily he will be able to avoid the sin even at the price of great sacrifice — though the Church's unequivocal prohibition should alone suffice for the faithful, since obedience to a divine command does not depend on one's understanding the reason for it.

The second group's opposition to the Pope's encyclical is motivated by a general amoralism and a resentful rebellion against the Church and her teaching authority and it must therefore be judged very differently. Unfortunately, there are many priests in this group also. And because of the hardships it imposes on many married couples, the encyclical affords this group a welcome occasion for undermining respect for the Holy Father as well as faith in the teaching authority of the Holy Church among those who otherwise have been resisting the poison of secularization.

It is therefore of the utmost importance for everyone who rightly resists any presentation of marriage as a mere means of procreation to understand that the momentous complement the Second Vatican Council set forth to the past presentation of the essence and value of marriage neither makes artificial birth control permissible nor blurs the difference between it and the observance of rhythm.[2]

But one must be careful not to obscure with mistaken arguments the true reasons — clearly brought forward in the encyclical *Humanae Vitae* — for the sinfulness of artificial birth control. This is important for those who want to defend the encyclical.

I shall therefore attempt to shed light on the meaning and value of marriage in all its depth and grandeur as well as on the mysterious connection of this love-communion with procreation. Then, after elaborating the true reasons why artificial birth control is sinful, we shall reply to some specific objections made against the encyclical.

---

2. *Pastoral Constitution on the Church in the Modern World,* 48ff. This emphasis on love in marriage is founded not only in Scripture, but also in many official utterances of the Church as well as in the decrees of Trent (Denzinger 1797-1799). This development of the meaning and value of marriage was beautifully expressed by Pius XII in certain of his addresses.

# Part I

# SEX, LOVE, AND MARRIAGE

# 1. MARRIAGE AS A COMMUNITY OF LOVE

The very meaning and value which marriage possesses of its own cannot be understood if we fail to start from the central reality of the love between man and woman. And here, let us be frank, we touch on what used to be a kind of scandal in Catholic writings on marriage. One heard much of the *will* of the flesh, the remedy for concupiscence, and mutual help and assistance, but one heard very little of love. We mean the love between man and woman, the deepest source of natural happiness in human life, the great, glorious love of which the Canticle of Canticles says: "If a man shall give all the substance of his house for love, he shall despise it as nothing."

In contradistinction to the general silence concerning this love, Pope Pius XII was eloquent:

> The charm exercised by human love has been for centuries the inspiring theme of admirable works of genius, in literature, in music, in the visual arts; a theme always old and always new, upon which the ages have embroidered, without ever exhausting it, the most elevated and poetic variations.[3]

---

3. *The Pope Speaks*, ed. Michael Chinigo (New York: Pantheon, 1957).

It is shocking that in the past the real, valid motive for marriage has been for the most part overlooked, that the intrinsic relation of this type of love to a full mutual self-donation in bodily union has been ignored. Compared with this great, noble, and basic incentive, which the Canticle of Canticles says "is strong as death," the isolated desire of the flesh is superficial and secondary. Who can deny that it is this love which shakes the soul of man to its very depths, which marks the deepest experience in the natural realm of human life? Certainly, there is a broad scale in the potential of men for love, in the depth and completeness of love. Leonardo da Vinci said: "The greater the man, the deeper his love." Great loves, such as that between Leonore and Florestan in Beethoven's *Fidelio,* or St. Elisabeth of Hungary and her husband, or St. Louis of France and his wife, may be rare and presuppose great and deep personalities, but in every human being who has ever experienced a real love, limited and imperfect as it may be, it is the great, dynamic human experience in his life.

If we wish to understand the nature of spousal love, this glorious heritage of paradise, and the God-willed valid aspect of the sexual sphere, we should read the Canticle of Canticles open-mindedly. We should not think of the analogical meaning, but take it in its original literal sense; then we can breathe the atmosphere of this love, and see the sublimity of bodily union when experienced as the ultimate God-given mutual self-donation. And, when we have grasped the beauty of the literal sense, we should consider the implication of the fact that the Liturgy uses it as an analogy for the relation of the soul to God, and uses it in the Office of the Blessed Virgin. Should it not be clear that only something which is noble on the human level can be used as an analogy for the supernatural relation of the soul to Christ? Why does the sacred author use this relation and not that of friendship, such as the one uniting David and Jonathan?

## 2. ERRORS CONCERNING MARRIAGE

### Puritanical distrust of spousal love

Some Catholic authors in undertaking to praise spousal love deprive it of its ecstatic ardor, of its splendor and unique *intentio unionis* (desire for union), thus detaching it consistently from the sexual sphere, from the bodily union; others, again, look down on spousal love and interpret its ecstatic character, its unique splendor, as a mirage, an illusion. Some ten years ago a famous Catholic philosopher even went so far as to claim that this type of love is nothing but a disguised sex instinct and that only in so far as *agape* exists between the spouses does their relationship deserve to be called authentic love. Most Catholic authors in the past, however, ignored the existence of this love entirely, simply omitting it when speaking of marriage.

It cannot be stated with sufficient emphasis that the time has come for us to do away with the gnostic and puritanical suspicion of spousal love, love in the most specific sense, of which the Canticle of Canticles speaks in such a unique way.

Let us be existential; let us see that the love between man and woman is a specific category and type of love, even if we prescind from the sphere of sex, that it is a beautiful and glorious reality which is destined by God's will to play a fundamental role in man's life, and that this love is the classical motive for marriage, that marriage is precisely the fulfillment of this love.

And it is this love which we call "spousal love."

## Misunderstanding of the sexual as mere instinct

Still another basic error bars the way to the understanding of the true meaning and value of marriage. Every approach to the sphere of sex in man which considers it a mere subdivision of the realm of instincts and biological urges having no intrinsic relation to the spiritual sphere, like thirst and the need of sleep, the meaning of which is to be found in an extrinsic end which they serve, is bound to prevent an understanding of the true nature and meaning of sex. As soon as we assume that the nature and the meaning of sex in man can be treated as a mere biological reality, we have blinded ourselves to the mystery of the sphere of sex — to the meaning and value which it can have, on the one hand, and the terrible moral evil of impurity, on the other.

If sex were really nothing more than a biological instinct, such as thirst or hunger, it would be incomprehensible why the satisfaction of an instinct implanted in man's nature by God should be something immoral outside of marriage, especially if it led to procreation. To consider the sexual sphere as a subdivision of instincts is to reduce the immorality of impurity to the mere violation of a positive commandment.

We cannot grasp the mystery embodied in this sphere until we grasp that its deepest meaning consists in being a unique fulfillment of spousal love and its desire for union. We must realize that this sphere is essentially ordained toward the constitution of a lasting, irrevocable union, the union to which spousal love aspires, and which is sanctioned by God; only then can we grasp the real sinfulness of every isolation of the satisfaction of sexual desire from the constitution of this God-sanctioned union. Only when we understand that the sexual act implies a mutual, irrevocable self-donation and is by its very nature called and destined to constitute an indissoluble union, can we see the desecration involved in sexual satisfaction outside of marriage.

## Spousal love as "forma" of the sexual sphere and the Freudian error of reversing this truth

Freud dealt with the sexual sphere as the primary reality, which can be understood in itself without recurring to spousal love and which offers us the key to the nature of love. This was one of his great and fatal errors. Therefore, I dare say that notwithstanding all his valuable contributions to psychopathology, he was blind not only to the nature of love — that even a child can see — but also to the nature of sex; for this sphere reveals its true character, meaning, depth, and mystery only when seen in the light of spousal love, as a field of fulfillment of the lasting, irrevocable union in which "two become one flesh." There is irony in the fact that although Freud tried to reduce everything to sex, he failed to understand the very nature of sex.

However, the notion that the sexual constitutes in itself a primary reality, an autonomous sphere, a subdivision of the sphere of instincts, is unfortunately not restricted to Freud. In a different form we find this error in every conception of sexual desire which sees in it primarily an expression of concupiscence, the lust of the flesh, an evil in itself, at best tolerated when serving the end of procreation and when legitimated in marriage.

In this conception, also, the meaning of the sexual sphere, its true value, is completely overlooked, because it is severed from its mission to constitute a unique, irrevocable union between two persons to which the love of man and woman aspires and in which it finds its fulfillment.

To quote Pope Pius XII again:

> The conjugal act, in its natural structure, is a personal action, a simultaneous and immediate cooperation of husband and wife, which, owing to the very nature of the agents and the propriety of the act, is the expression of the reciprocal gift, which, according to the word of Scripture, effects the union "in one flesh." [4]

We could also apply to the conjugal act the admirable words of St. Ambrose in speaking of the kiss: "Those who kiss one another are not content with the donation of their lips, but want to breathe their very souls into each other."

---

4. Ibid.

### 3. THE VALUE OF SEX AS THE EXPRESSION AND FULFILLMENT OF SPOUSAL LOVE AND THE SIN OF ISOLATING IT

We must, finally, free ourselves from seeing in the bodily union something evil, for the toleration of which in marriage one must desperately try to find a reason. We must learn to see that the bodily union, destined to be the fulfillment of spousal love and an ultimate mutual self-donation, is as such something noble and a great mystery, a sacred land which we should approach with deep reverence and never without a specific sanction of God; and that precisely because of this nobility and sacred mystery, because of the great value which it is destined to realize, every abuse is a terrible sin, and even contains something sacrilegious.

In stressing that it is a grave error to see the sexual sphere and the sexual act as something evil as such, we are far from denying that the isolation of the sexual sphere is not only a theoretical error but a widespread tendency of our fallen nature. The sexual sphere has also, when isolated and separated from spousal love and the mutual self-donation in marriage, an enormous attractive power. The danger of being caught and seduced by this aspect of the sexual sphere is indeed a great one and it lurks in the greater part of mankind. In my book *In Defense of Purity* I have dealt at length with this powerful fascination.[5] Whenever anyone gives in to it and undertakes to satisfy an isolated sexual desire, we are confronted with the grave sin of impurity, an

---

5. Baltimore: Helicon Press, 1962.

outgrowth of evil concupiscence and a desecration. This sin includes a mysterious betrayal of our spiritual nature. But this in no way entitles us to look at the act of bodily union as something evil. It becomes evil through its isolation. Precisely because it is something noble, deep, and mysterious in its God-ordained relation to two becoming one flesh in the sublime love union of marriage, its abuse is a terrible desecration. To conclude that something is evil as such because its abuse constitutes a terrible sin and because in our fallen nature the tendency for such abuse is great is obviously completely illogical. Should we look on intellectual work and scholarship as something evil in itself, because it certainly produces in many persons a proud attitude, because it fosters pride? Or should we see in reason something evil because of the danger of rationalism?

No! Great and terrible as is the danger of impurity, true as it is that in our nature there lurks the tendency to respond to the appeal of the isolation of sex, this in no way alters the fact that the valid, real meaning of this sphere is to be a field of fulfillment for spousal love and that the original, valid aspect of the marital act is its function of being a mutual self-donation in the sacred bond of marriage, the constitution of an irrevocable union, and that it is thus as such not something evil, but on the contrary something great, noble, and pure.

Thus, instead of saying that the sinful satisfaction of sexual desire becomes legitimate through marriage, we should say that the sexual act, because it is destined to be the consummation of this sublime union and the fulfillment of spousal love, becomes sinful when desecrated by isolation.

## 4. MARRIAGE AS "REMEDIUM CONCUPISCENTIAE"

This does not contradict St. Paul's recommendation of marriage also as a remedy for concupiscence — given the fact that in many persons the isolated sexual desire threatens to lead them to sin, that is, to desecrate the bodily union. Of this desecration St. Paul says: "Or do you not know that he who cleaves to a harlot becomes one body with her?" Marriage, in which the bodily union serves the "becoming one flesh," can also be a remedy for concupiscence. But the *ut avertatur peccatum,* that sin may be averted, is not a substitute for spousal love. It means only that the one who is tormented by temptations of an isolated sexual desire should rather marry than remain unwed. But it does not mean that it would be superfluous for him to find a person whom he loves, because it belongs to this "remedy" that, to the greatest extent possible, the marital act become the expression of spousal love and the constitution of a lasting, irrevocable bond.

## 5. FALSE REACTION TO THE PURITANICAL SUSPICION OF MARRIAGE: IDOLIZATION OF SEXUAL PLEASURE

Many Catholics consider the widespread positive attitude to the sexual sphere a great advance over the puritanical prudery and hypocrisy of the Victorian age. But incomparably worse than the puritanical attitude, in which the sexual act as such was considered base and evil, is the currently fashionable opinion that experience of sexual pleasure belongs to "self-fulfillment," that this pleasure is a divine gift which we should enjoy without restraint. This opinion falsifies the meaning and nature of the sexual sphere so radically that it becomes impossible to understand the meaning of the marriage act as the expression and fulfillment of wedded love, of mutual self-donation, of a union of love. The marriage act becomes even more degraded than in the puritanical view: the latter was at least recognizing its mysterious character when it considered sex a source of the mystery of iniquity, whereas in the contemporary view sex is considered a mere means of pleasure. In my book *In Defense of Purity* I have described two negative aspects which are found in the sexual sphere in addition to the aspects willed by God. The puritanical position saw in the sexual sphere only the two negative aspects, overlooking the positive character which discloses itself only in the light of spousal love. But the opinion current today separates pleasure from its function of serving the love union and makes it an end in itself; stripped thereby of all its depth, sex is even more misunderstood than in the Puritanical view.

Moreover, the term "love" is completely misused by many Catholics. They are blind to the nature of spousal love and attempt to reduce it to "sex-appeal." Even when some admit that sexual intercourse without love is something negative, love is in fact taken to mean something completely peripheral, basically a sensual desire, which lacks all the characteristics of love in general as well as those of spousal love in particular. It is of the greatest importance to stress that the question of birth control must be considered in the light of the mystery of true love and its fulfillment in bodily donation and never in terms of sexual attraction — today so often called "love." For isolated sexual pleasure is often — as in the widely circulated discussion of the encyclical *Humanae Vitae* by the German Professor Fritz Leist — thought to be the motive for marriage. (This consistently leads to the defense of promiscuity — under the title of "pre-marital relations" or "trial marriage" — and of homosexuality as a source of self-fulfilling pleasure.) This will become clearer when we briefly reflect on the distinctive marks of spousal love — that is, of love between man and woman.

## 6. ESSENTIAL DIFFERENCES BETWEEN TRUE SPOUSAL LOVE AND ISOLATED SEXUAL DESIRE

Many say: The sexual drive is obviously the specific mark of spousal love since this type of love presupposes the difference between the sexes. To that I reply: Certainly, but the difference between man and woman is not purely biological. After all, in the spiritual sphere there is also a complementary difference. In an essay, "Friendship between the Sexes," which appeared in my book *Man and Woman,* I treat of this spiritual, complementary difference, this specifically spiritual fecundation of each other, this completion of man and woman, which creates a special situation.[6] Indeed, it is no accident that great men saints have often found in women their most faithful and understanding followers, and conversely.

Spousal love is also characterized by another

---

6. *Man and Woman* (Chicago: Franciscan Herald Press, 1965; paperback - Chicago: Henry Regnery Company, 1968).

mark, namely, that the *intentio unionis* contained in every love, the longing to participate in the life of the beloved, the longing for a special type of communion, reaches its high point here. In every love we hasten spiritually to the other; in every love we turn to him to encounter him fully as a person and we yearn for a requital of love — for a real communion between personal beings is possible only when we look into one another in this reciprocal gaze characteristic of love. Only in love do we present our countenance fully to the other and truly disclose ourselves to him. And this attains a totally new character in spousal love. This love aims at marriage, and I am not as yet thinking of bodily union but of the union of two individual lives. Surely it is an awesome thing that two human beings want to lead *one* life, that they wish to live together, to carry one name, that they unite their lives and share everything with each other! Spousal love is also characterized by the fact that it is the purest I-thou communion. In *Metaphysik der Gemeinschaft*[7] I distinguish these two fundamental dimensions of communion: the I-thou communion, where two persons stand face to face, and the we-communion, where persons stand side by side and turn together toward a third object. These two dimensions of communion are normally present to a certain degree in every relationship, but the relationship is characterized according to the dimension that is dominant and proper to it. I would say that, in general, friendship is a we-communion where persons

---

7. Regensburg, Germany: Habbel, 1954.

stand side by side and together turn toward common goods and values and share mutual interests. In spousal love, on the contrary, love itself is specifically the theme. Here, an explicit I-thou situation predominates, always with the longing for the attainment of the ultimate union in the mutual interpenetration of souls in love. Naturally, this implies that the beloved person as well as the mutual love becomes thematic in a unique way.

Still another mark of spousal love must be discussed — namely, what we call "being-in-love." This expression is so often misused that some believe that this is really nothing else but being sexually attracted to another. But this is an unfortunate error. The point here is that there are two radically divergent phenomena. Certainly, being in love includes the fact that the charm of the other sex discloses itself in a unique manner in the beloved. The shining forth of the beauty and mystery of the feminine as such to the man and of the masculine as such to the woman belongs to the state of being in love. Indeed, these are embodied in the beloved, in him alone. The decisive point is that in the true state of being in love the charm of the other sex is exclusively embodied in the beloved, as Petrarch says so beautifully of Laura, *che sola a me par donna* (who alone seems woman to me). This mark of being in love is the clearest antithesis to "sex-appeal," to mere sexual attraction. Regarding the other only as sexually fascinating and experiencing an isolated sensual desire represents a phenomenon radically different from the true state of being in love. In this state the beloved stands before us as something immeasurably precious; his beauty awakens reverence in us. We are not yet referring to an especially deep being-in-love, but only to the phenomenon of being-in-love as such. Anyone who is truly in love gazes upon the other with the awareness that "I am not worthy of her," although with his whole heart he hopes that his love may be requited.

As long as I find someone only sexually attractive, as long as this person awakens only sexual desire in me, I in no way look up to him because of this. In the case of truly being in love, I am drawn into a dimension of depth, I become more sensitive and more reverent. In the case of isolated sensual desire, where I find someone merely enticing, I am drawn into the periphery. I even become less sensitive, less reverent. In the true state of being in love the beloved stands before me as a person in a unique way. I take him fully seriously as a person. In a mere sensual attraction the partner is an object for my satisfaction. In the case of truly being in love the whole charm of the other sex is embodied in the one beloved person, whereas in sensual desire the other is just *one* good representative of the other sex among many. The other is only one example that I happen to find. The real state of being-in-love — as long as it really lasts — possesses absolute exclusiveness. It is impossible, from the purely psychological point of view, to be in love with two people at the same time. This psychological exclusiveness (we are not yet touching the moral question) is grounded in the essence of "being in love." In the mere sexual attraction to the charm of a person we do not find the least trace of this exclusiveness. On the contrary, it is accompanied by the thought: this one today, tomorrow another, *delectat variatio.* This attitude is typically represented by Don Juan in Mozart's marvelous opera; he says to Leporello: "I would be unfaithful to the female sex were I to attach myself to one." This is the most emphatic antithesis to being in love. Here the female species is the specific theme and then only under the aspect of unalloyed sexual allurement. Every individual woman is merely an example of the species woman. For the person in love, on the contrary, the charm of the other sex can fully unfold itself only in the individual personality of the beloved; only thanks to his whole personality does the charm begin to glow and speak in its mysterious radiance, only against the background of all the other personal values of the one he loves. Needless to say, the quality of the sensual is entirely different in these two cases. (When I speak of sensual appeal, I have in mind the whole sphere of the sexual and whatever is psychologically and spiritually connected with it.) In the case of the person truly in love, the mystery of sex shows its true face in all its depth, in its mysteriousness which calls for reverence, in its moving quality, because it is formed by love; in the other case, we have only a caricature of the mystery of sex, because sex is isolated and separated from the spiritual person. With this caricature there inevitably goes a de-personalization. Whoever is seized by sheer sexual desire is himself de-personalized; he does not act as a person in that moment. Also, the one to whom he turns is not considered as a person, but is treated as a thing.

How much more noble and reverent, more aware, and consequently more lovable is a man made by love! How much richer the cosmos becomes for him and how he is led even to a greater religious depth! For one truly in love the sun shines more brightly, nature becomes more beautiful, his entire life is elevated to a higher plane. The person is then loosed from the shackles of habit which so dominate us, becomes emancipated from the dangers of conventionality, awakens much more to the hierarchy of values. The Canticle of Canticles expresses this when it says that the man who would give up all the possessions of his house for his love would regard the sacrifice as *nothing*.

Thus, we see how false it is to confuse the true state of being in love with isolated sexual attraction. And it is important to recognize that the terms "love" and "being in love" today often denote two *completely antithetical* attitudes. Nowadays, we commonly hear such objections as: Certainly, I admit that there happen to be extraordinary men with a great capacity for loving; this is very beautiful indeed, but it is something I am not endowed with and therefore for me being in love is simply being sexually attracted by someone. To this we can answer that an extraordinary love, the love-potential of a Romeo, is not under discussion. Even a completely simple, undifferentiated man who in no way rises above the ordinary, if he falls in love once in his life, exhibits the essential characteristics of being in love which separate it from mere sexual craving. Even in this man the loving attitude will be an experience completely different from an isolated sexual desire. In the latter instance, he will not at all think of uniting his life with that of the other; he will not think of marriage.

Still another element to be stressed in spousal love

is the unparalleled happiness which is the fruit of
this love. The mere ability to love bestows a singular
happiness, not to mention the great happiness of
love requited and of the union it results in. But this
should not mislead one into believing that he can
seek the happiness of love as an end for which the
partner is a mere means. The authentic happiness
of love is in reality a gift superabundantly granted.
In the very instant in which he sees the other person as a mere means to happiness, he no longer
loves and thus *cannot attain* the happiness proper
to love.

There are many things which are ruined from the
outset when they are considered in a means-to-an-
end relationship. They must be taken seriously in
themselves. If I listen to a Beethoven Symphony only
because I wish to experience a wonderful feeling,
I will then experience nothing. I must be focused
on the symphony and immerse myself in its beauty;
I must forget myself; and so it is in love. One should
not forget that happiness is a result of love and not
the motive for love. The motive for love is the
preciousness, the beauty, the goodness which the
other possesses, the value of this unique personality
in its entire beauty. Love is a value response. But in
all isolated sexual desire the opposite is true: the
sham-happiness of mere sexual pleasure can be
directly pursued and the other person can be considered exclusively as a means.

Spousal love alone constitutes the organic link to
the sensual sphere, a sphere essentially foreign to
every other love, such as friendship, the love of a
mother, the love of a child. This does not exclude
that in fact sexual instincts oftentimes creep into

other types of love. But in such cases it is always more or less a perversion or at least a foreign body that has been added and not something which is in its very quality and nature ordered to be an organic fulfillment and expression of that love. Everyone who has an understanding of the nature and quali- tative character of love and of sex, and who has not fallen prey to unrealistic abstract theories having a mythological character, such as Freud's pan-sexu- alism, can clearly see that it is only spousal love which has this organic relation to the sexual sphere. Spousal love is organically connected with it and finds in this sphere in a special way its expression and fulfillment. The mystery enclosed in this sphere possesses an incomparable depth.[8] In a certain sense the sexual in every man is his "personal secret." There is therefore a profound significance in the fact that the Biblical word "to know" also signifies the marital act. Thus, the marital act is an ultimate self- donation, a giving of self. And because this sphere possesses a unique mysteriousness, it can become the vehicle and expression and fulfillment not only of the union desired by love, but also of the full and irrevocable mutual consent to become one — that is, of the clearly expressed *will* to an indissoluble union and bond, a will which organically grows out of love and which can in no way be separated from it if this spousal love is really present. This will can appear without it in marriages misleadingly labeled "marriages of convenience" (made for finan- cial and other considerations). The mutual consent

---

8. See *In Defense of Purity.*

of the will (the *consensus*) to unite can therefore be given without love, but true spousal love can never be separated from the desire for this *consensus,* for the explicit and permanent bond.

We must therefore reject the application of the words "love" and "being in love" to an "abandonment" motivated by mere isolated sexual attraction, where in reality the individual flings himself away. This is a desecration of the mystery of sex, turning it into the *mysterium iniquitatis* of impurity. Such an isolated sexual desire is the exact antithesis to true love.

It should thus be clear that the grave error of seeing the primary, valid aspect of the sexual sphere as a mere realm of instincts is not corrected when, as at times today, people urge that it be considered something positive, while still overlooking the fact that its essential meaning is the fulfillment of spousal love. Whether one sees sexual desire in a positive or in a negative light is not the decisive point. One must see that this instinct is precisely not destined to remain an instinct like other instincts, but to become an expression of spousal love and an ultimate self-donation serving the union of both spouses. And even if one sees it merely as something parallel to the spiritual union, a kind of analogy in the bodily sphere, one still remains blind to the mystery, to the high value of the *mysterium unionis* and to the *mysterium iniquitatis* in its abuse.

## 7. PRUDISHNESS, NEUTRAL ATTITUDE OR REVERENCE AND MODESTY?

This character of mystery is especially overlooked today, and many proclaim it to be a great step for-

ward that instead of a puritanical reticence, one now
speaks in an open and neutral manner of this sphere.
In reality, this is no progress at all. Little as the
prudish attitude does justice to this sphere, the neutral attitude does still less.

The right antithesis to the puritan attitude is the
reverent approach to this sphere in its character of
mystery which excludes by its very essence every
neutralization. It is erroneous to believe that a sense
of shame can only indicate a response to something
negative, for there are different types of shame; for
instance, a virtuous man will want to hide his face
when he is publicly praised. There is one kind, a
noble modesty, which is a response to the intimate
and mysterious character of a thing; and to misin-
terpret this bashfulness and modesty, which is called
for in the sphere of sex, as mere prudery, is to ex-
hibit the same deplorable blindness and superfi-
ciality which confuses humility with servility, and
purity with frigidity. Indeed, this neutralization reveals the most disastrous failure to understand this
sphere in its ecstatic and mysterious character and its
essential intimacy.

## 8. SPOUSAL LOVE AND THE IRREVOCABLE UNION OF MARRIAGE

We must thus start with an understanding of the
meaning and value of marriage as the closest love
union between man and woman, as constituting the
most intimate human I-thou communion, the irrevocable bond which Christ elevated to a sacrament.

This union is constituted by the consensus of the
spouses — that is, the lifelong mutual self-donation is
constituted by the expressed will of the partners,

solemnly pronounced before God and thereby, as it were, entrusted to God. The *intentio unionis* of spousal love finds its valid expression in this consensus and its fulfillment in the irrevocable union constituted by this consensus. It reaches, however, a still new fulfillment in the conjugal act, in the consummation of the marriage, with the full, accomplished self-donation, whereby they become "two in one flesh." Who can fail to grasp the grandeur and beauty of marriage and the bodily union which it essentially implies if he contemplates without prejudice the words of the Lord referring to the indissolubility of marriage?

> Because of the hardness of your heart he wrote you that precept. But from the beginning of the creation God made them male and female. For this cause a man shall leave his father and mother, and cleave to his wife, and the two shall become one flesh. Therefore now they are no longer two, but one flesh. What therefore God has joined together, let no man put asunder (Mark 10, 5-9).

Not the slightest connotation is to be found in these words which would justify a suspicious attitude toward love or the bodily union. That the bodily union is seen as the fulfillment of love clearly appears from the emphasis on the becoming one and the mutual self-donation. No mention is made of procreation. The words of Genesis clearly refer to this love: "Wherefore a man shall leave father and mother" (Gen. 2; 24). And the sublime words in which the indissolubility of marriage is expressed, "What therefore God has joined together, let no man put asunder," clearly disclose the depth and grandeur of the union constituted by the marital act: this love union was sealed by God and therefore it is not dissoluble by man. No unprejudiced mind can read and understand these words, receive them in all their solemnity in his soul, without being aware of the abyss which separates this conception of marriage from the gnostic, puritan approach so often found among Catholics.

## 9. THE SUPERNATURAL TRANSFORMATION OF MARRIAGE

And does not the fact that Christ granted to marriage the dignity of a sacrament, which means not only something sacred but also a source of special graces, disclose the high meaning and value of marriage?

It is not possible within the framework of this brief work to broach the most sublime aspect of marriage as a sacrament. But we wish to stress that spousal love also is called to be transformed by Christ; indeed, only in Christ and through Christ can the spouses live up to the full glory and depth to which this love by its very nature aspires. As Pius XII stated:

> But what new and unutterable beauty is added to this love of two human hearts, when its song is harmonized with the hymn of two souls vibrating with supernatural life! Here, too, there is a mutual exchange of gifts; and then, through bodily tenderness and its healthy joys, through natural affection and its impulses, through a spiritual union and its delights, the two beings who love each other identify themselves in all that is most intimate in them, from the unshaken depths of their beliefs to the highest summit of their hopes.[9]

---

9. Allocution to newlyweds, 23 Oct. 1940.

The transformation of spousal love by Christ does not, however, make it lose its specific feature of spousal love. To quote the late Pontiff again:

> God with His love neither destroys nor changes nature, but perfects it; and St. Francis de Sales, who well knew the human heart, concluded his beautiful page on the sacred character of conjugal love with this twofold advice: "Keep, O husbands, a tender, constant, and cordial love for your wives . . . . And you, wives, love tenderly, cordially . . . the husbands whom God has given you."

> Cordiality and tenderness, then, from one side and from the other. "Love and faithfulness," he used to say, "always create intimacy and confidence; thus the saints were wont to give many demonstrations of affection in their marriages, demonstrations truly amorous, but chaste, tender, and sincere." [10]

_____

10. Ibid.

# Part II

# MARRIAGE AND PROCREATION

## 1. THE MEANING OF MARRIAGE AND THE PRINCIPLE OF SUPERABUNDANT FINALITY

To this sublime love union God has confided the coming into being of a new man, a cooperation with His divine creativity. Could we think of any thing more beautiful than this connection between the deepest love communion, the ultimate self-donation out of love, and the creation of a new human being? A deep mystery is here offered to us, which calls for reverence and awe. But we can grasp the grandeur and depth of this connection only if we first understand the meaning and value of marriage as a love communion and the meaning and value of the marital act as the consummation of this ultimate union to which spousal love aspires. We can appreciate the mysterious character of the link between the marital act and the birth of a new person only if we have understood its finality as an instance of the principle of superabundance and not as an instrumental finality in which the conjugal act is looked at as a mere means for procreation. And it must be most emphatically stated that understanding the meaning and value of marriage as a love union *does not minimize but rather enhances the link between marriage and procreation.*

This will become clear as we examine briefly the nature of the principle of superabundance and its difference from merely instrumental finality.

We cannot deny that one end of knowledge is to enable man to act; our entire practical life, from the most primitive activities to the most complicated ones, presupposes knowledge. Moreover, a still more sublime end of knowledge is to enable us to attain the moral perfection and sanctification which is the presupposition for our eternal welfare. And yet, if these can rightly be called the ends to which knowledge is destined, knowledge has undoubtedly also a meaning and value of its own; and the relation to the ends it serves has the character of super-abundance. This is a typical case of a finality in which the end is not the exclusive *raison d'être* of something.

This kind of finality differs patently from the instrumental finality which is in question when we call a surgical instrument a means for operating, or money a means for procuring ourselves a good, or teeth a means for the mastication of food. The main difference between instrumental finality and the finality that we have called the principle of super-abundance consists in the fact that in instrumental finality the being which is considered as a means is in its meaning and value completely dependent upon the end, whereas in superabundant finality, it has a meaning and value independently of the end to which it leads.

In the instrumental finality the *causa finalis* de-termines the *causa formalis;* in the superabundant the *causa formalis* differs from the *causa finalis.*

In the case of a knife, the end (cutting) determines its entire nature; its meaning is identical with serving this end, and its value depends upon its function as a means. Its only *raison d'être* is to be a means for cutting. This is a typical instrumental finality.

In instrumental finality, the end is the exclusive *raison d'être* of the means; in superabundant finality, the good serving the end has also a *raison d'être* in itself.

We saw above that the intrinsic meaning and value of marriage consists in its being the deepest and closest love union. We saw that in its mutual self-donation and in its constitution of a matchless union, the conjugal act has the meaning of a unique fulfillment of spousal love. But to that high good, which has a meaning and value in itself, has been entrusted procreation. The same act, which in its meaning is the constitution of the union, has been superabundantly made the source of procreation; thus, we must speak of procreation as the end — but not in the sense of mere instrumental finality. Though we may consider the sexual instinct in animals as a mere means for the continuation of the species, as an end in the sense of an instrumental finality, this is patently impossible with respect to the love between man and woman or to their union in marriage.

Occasionally, it has been conceded that in their subjective approach the spouses need not look at marriage and the conjugal union as a mere means in the instrumental sense; but the claim continues to be made that objectively the relation between a union of love and procreation has the character of an instrumental finality. It is claimed that God has implanted in their hearts the love between man and woman and the desire for a conjugal union as a mere means for procreation. But in arguing thus, one has not understood the real character of the link between marriage and procreation.

We touch here on a general and dangerous tendency to overlook the very nature of the person and to assume that the kind of instrumentality that is to be found in the biological realm can be extended to the spiritual realm of man. As long as instincts or urges are in question, their inner logic and *ratio* goes, so to speak, over the head of the person. It is true that neither man's intelligence nor his free will establishes the meaningful direction of an instinct such as thirst or the desire to sleep. God has given to these instincts and urges their meaningfulness without involving man's intelligence; this finality is similar to the one found in merely unconscious physiological processes. In so far as the experienced urge or instinct of thirst, for instance, is at stake, we thus rightly say that its *raison d'être* is to procure for the body the necessary liquid, and that God has installed it as a means to that end.

But when it comes to the spiritual acts of the person, such as willing or loving or experiencing contrition, we can no longer assume that in the eyes of God they have no meaning in themselves but are only means linked to an end by a finality similar to that of the instincts or urges. We must not forget that God takes man as person so seriously that He has addressed Himself to man, and that it depends on man's free response whether or not he will attain his eternal destiny. St. Augustine expressed this when he wrote: "He who made you without you, will not justify you without you." The spiritual attitudes of man have a meaning and a *ratio* in themselves, and they can never be treated as having their real significance independently of the person; they involve a person's intelligence and his freedom, his capacity to respond meaningfully, and not an impersonal, automatic finality going over the person's head. Consequently, it is impossible to see them as having their real significance beyond and independently of the person's conscious experience. Man is not a puppet for God, but a personal being to whom God addresses Himself and from whom He expects a meaningful response.

This devalorization and degradation of the spiritual human attitudes is incompatible with the character of man as a person, his character of *imago Dei;* it ignores the very fact that God has revealed Himself to man and also the way in which man's redemption took place.

It may be objected: Does not God often use an evil attitude as a means for something good in the life of the individual and especially in the history of mankind? May not an attitude which is evil in itself become a means leading to something good? Yes, indeed, but the *felix culpa* does not remove from the fault its morally negative character and does not entitle us to look at a moral decision as something which acquires its real meaning only in its possible function as *felix culpa,* instead of seeing its primary meaning in its moral value or disvalue.

The kind of finality which we have in mind when we say that God's providence makes out of evil something leading to a good differs obviously also in a radical way from the instrumental finality with which we are confronted in the biological sphere. It is not a finality which is rooted in the nature of something, but a free intervention of God's providence, using something in a direction which is even opposed to its nature and meaning. It would obviously make no sense to say that the end of moral evil is to lead to something good; that would be to claim that the very nature of a moral fault makes it a means for bringing about a good. The *culpa* is as such *infelix,* and that it may become *felix* is owing to an intervention of God, which never entitles us to say that this is the objective, valid meaning of moral guilt in God's eyes. God does not judge man according to whether or not his sins later on prove to be a *felix culpa* but according to their intrinsic sinfulness. Thus, we see that the merciful intervention of God, making a good grow out of evil, in no way reduces the role of man to that of a puppet.

## 2. THE MEANING OF MARRIAGE AND ITS PRIMARY END

Coming back to our topic, we must state that it is incompatible with the very nature of the person to consider the deepest human spiritual experiences as mere subjective aspects of something that, in God's eyes, is a means for an extrinsic end. It would be seeing man in a merely biological light if we assumed that love between man and woman, the highest earthly good, is a mere means for the conservation of the species, that its objective *raison d'être* is exclusively to instigate a union which serves procreation. The God-given, essential link between love of man and woman and its fulfillment in the marital union, on the one hand, and the creation of a new person, on the other hand, has precisely the character of superbundance, which is a much deeper connection than would be one of merely instrumental finality.

But let it be stated again emphatically: to stress the meaning and value of marriage as the most intimate, indissoluble union of love does not contradict the doctrine that procreation is the primary end of marriage. The distinction we have made between meaning and end, as well as the insight that marriage has a value of its own besides its sublime value as source of procreation, in no way diminishes the importance of the link between marriage and procreation; it rather enhances the link and places it in the right perspective.

## 3. WHY ARTIFICIAL BIRTH CONTROL IS SINFUL

We can now see more clearly the difference between natural and artificial birth control. The sinfulness of artificial birth control is rooted in the arrogation of the right to separate the actualized love union in marriage from a possible conception, to sever the wonderful, deeply mysterious connection instituted by God. This mystery is approached in an irreverent attitude. We are here confronted with the fundamental sin of irreverence toward God, the denial of our creaturehood, the acting as if we were our own lords. This is a basic denial of the *religio,* of our being bound to God; it is a disrespect for the mysteries of God's creation, and its sinfulness increases with the rank of the mystery in question. It is the same sinfulness that lies in suicide or in

euthanasia, in both of which we act as if we were
masters of life.

Every *active* intervention of the spouses that elim-
inates the possibility of conception through the conjugal act is incompatible with the holy mystery of
the superabundant relation in this incredible gift of
God. And this irreverence also affects the purity of
the conjugal act, because the union can be the real
fulfillment of love only when it is approached with
reverence and when it is embedded in the *religio,*
the consciousness of our basic bond to God.

To the sublime link between marriage and procreation Christ's words on the marriage bond also
apply: "What God has joined together, let no man
put asunder." This becomes still clearer when we
consider that the mystery of the birth of a man not
only should[11] be essentially linked to wedded love
(through the conjugal act, which is destined to be
the expression and fulfillment of this love), but is
always linked to a creative intervention of God.
Neither wedded love nor, still less, the physiological
process of conception is *itself capable* of creating a
human being with an immortal soul. On this point
Pope Paul VI quotes the encyclical *Mater et Magis-
tra*: " 'Human life is holy,' Pope John XXIII re-
minds us, 'and from conception on it demands the
immediate intervention of God!' " (*Humanae Vitae,*
13). Man always comes forth directly from the hand
of God, and therefore there is a unique and intimate relation between God and the spouses in the

---

11. See under 5 below, "The Order of What Is and the
    Order of What Ought to Be in Marriage."

act of procreation. In a fruitful conjugal act we can say that the spouses participate in God's act of creation; the conjugal act of the spouses is incorporated into the creative act of God and acquires a serving function in relation to His act.

We thus see that artificial birth control is sinful not only because it severs the mysterious link between the most intimate love union and the coming into existence of a new human being, but also because in a certain way it artificially cuts off the creative intervention of God, or better still, it artificially separates an act which is ordained toward co-operation with the creative act of God from this its destiny. For, as Paul VI says, this is to consider oneself not a servant of God, but the "Lord over the origin of human life" (*Humanae Vitae,* 13).

This irreverence, however, is exclusively limited to *active* intervention severing the conjugal act from its possible link with procreation.

The conjugal act does not in any way lose its full meaning and value when one knows that a conception is out of the question, as when age, or an operation for the sake of health, or pregnancy excludes it. The knowledge that a conception is not possible does not in the least taint the conjugal act with irreverence. In such cases, if the act is an expression of a deep love, anchored in Christ, it will rank even higher in its quality and purity than one that leads to a conception in a marriage in which the love is less deep and not formed by Christ. And even when for good and valid reasons conception should be avoided, the marital act in no way loses its *raison d'être,* because its meaning and value is the actualiz-

ation of the mutual self-donation of the spouses.[12]
The intention of avoiding conception does not imply irreverence as long as one does not actively interfere in order to cut the link between the conjugal act and a possible conception.

Nor is the practice of rhythm to avoid conception in any way irreverent, because the existence of rhythm — that is to say, the fact that conception is limited to a short period — is itself a God-given institution. In Section 6 we shall show in greater detail why the use of rhythm implies not the slightest irreverence or rebellion against God's institution of the wonderful link between the love union and procreation; it is in no way a subterfuge, as some Catholics tend to believe. On the contrary, it is a grateful acceptance of the possibility God has granted of avoiding conception — if this is legitimately desirable — without preventing the expression and fulfillment of spousal love in the bodily union.

## 4. TWO CONCEPTS OF NATURE IN "HUMANAE VITAE"

In order to understand the decisive difference between natural and artificial birth control we must be aware that the concept "nature" can have various meanings.

---

12. Even when conjugal love has grown cold, the marital act remains morally allowed, as long as worthily fulfilled and not desecrated by an impure attitude, since the right of the partner to one's body was granted in the marital consensus.

On the one hand, "nature" can signify the purely factual order of creation, especially material and biological creation. On the other, however, the same word can signify the essence of profoundly significant relations endowed with a high value.

That the time between the conception and birth of a man is nine months and not eight or ten months is merely a factual datum. It could just as well be otherwise, and this fact bears no significant value. That the openings of the esophagus and the windpipe are so close together in man that one can choke easily is certainly a fact, but it is not a deeply meaningful relation which has a value. On the contrary, injuries could be averted were this not the case. But quite different, for instance, is the fact that love brings happiness. This is not something merely factual; it is deeply meaningful and bears a high value. This is also true of the fact that a deep union of two persons is constituted in mutual love. Indeed, it is of meaning and value that this reciprocal love is the only path leading to a spiritual union that is much deeper and more authentic than any amalgamation, any fusion, in the impersonal world. This fact, which is rooted in the nature of love and the personal I-thou communion, is the bearer of a high value. No one can reasonably say that this fact could be otherwise. It could not be otherwise, because it is a significant, intelligible, and necessary intrinsic relation. Similarly, it would betray extraordinary value-blindness not to see the depth and sublimity of this relation, but to regard it as something indifferent.

However, the *essential* difference between the two concepts of nature is not that in the one case we

are confronted with an intelligible necessary fact
and in the other with a mere empirical fact, but
rather that in the one relations are deeply meaningful and possess a high *value,* and in the other they
are only factual.

It is certainly true that for the faithful Christian
both kinds of "nature" proceed from God and are
therefore reverently accepted. Nevertheless, nature in
the purely factual sense does not constitute something in which man ought not to intervene when
there are reasonable grounds for seeking a change
(in some circumstances he is even *obliged* to intervene). But intervention in nature in the second
sense, where meaning and value are grounded in
the essence of a thing, has a completely different
character. For this nature contains in its very meaning and value a unique message from God and calls
upon us to respect it.

This applies most of all to relations which constitute a deep mystery. Any violence done to these
is particularly presumptuous on the part of man the
creature. It is the usurpation of a right which man
does not possess; it reflects a desire to play the role
of God and Providence.

*The confusion of these two concepts of nature
has kept many from a proper understanding of the
encyclical Humanae Vitae.* They do not understand
that it is not a merely factual or exclusively biological connection but rather a great and sublime mystery that God has entrusted the generation of a
human being to the intimate union of man and
wife who love each other in wedded love and who
in becoming "two in one flesh" participate in the
creative act of God. This is gloriously expressed by

a prayer of an ancient Fulda ritual: "O Lord our God, who created man pure and spotless and thereafter ordained that in the propagation of the human race one generation should be produced from another by the *mystery of sweet love.*" The relation expressed here is thus not a merely factual one, but a staggering mystery, an ineffably deep and glorious fact. It is therefore a false argument to say: Why shouldn't man be allowed to regulate birth by artificial means, when God, after all, gave man control and dominion over nature and in the Old Testament made him the master of creation? Why is it allowed in medicine to take out the uterus, to transplant hearts, and perform many kinds of operations, but forbidden to intervene and modify nature in the case of the regulation of births? All those who argue in this way do not understand the radical difference between these two cases, because they confuse the two concepts of nature. As long as we remain within the realm of the purely "factual," we are not morally forbidden to intervene. But when we deal with meaningful relations which possess a high value in themselves, and when, as in this case, we deal with a mystery which we can contemplate only with the deepest reverence, then every artificial intervention is a flagrant moral wrong.

## A static or a dynamic concept of nature?

It is more than regrettable that the terms "dynamic" and "static" have been used in the polemic against the encyclical and its concept of nature. These typical shibboleths have taken on a particularly demagogic character in contemporary philosophical discussions. They appeal to irrational emotions and muddle the objective state of affairs. I have treated extensively the various confusions that lie behind these concepts in my book *Trojan Horse in the City of God*.[13]

## 5. THE RELATION BETWEEN BIOLOGICAL NATURE AND THE PERSON

One might object: [Co-operation in the creation of a new human being is, after all, confined to the *physical act*; this co-operation can even take place when no union of love is present; therefore, it is a purely biological datum; it is bound neither to reciprocal love nor to the consensus of marriage, and can even be the result of the crime of rape. ]

But this objection overlooks the deep connection between biological nature and the person, and in two ways. First, the fact that in human nature many things are *de facto* the result of physical processes does not in the least cancel the truth that these physical processes *should* be the expression of *spiritual* attitudes. Secondly, not everything that is *connected* with biological conditions is itself biological.

### The order of what is and the order of what ought to be in marriage

The *meaning* of the conjugal act is, as we have said, the ultimate fulfillment of the union desired by spousal love. It represents a unique gift of self, a gift that presupposes not only love, but also consensus — the volitional act necessarily aspired to by the type of love we termed spousal love and initiating the irrevocable bond of marriage. We have

---

13. Chicago: Franciscan Herald Press, 1968.

seen the grave sin in every profanation of the conjugal act, every isolation of it from mutual love and the consensus. This is the source of all *impurity*. On the other hand, the *active,* artificial isolation of this act from the possible generation of a human being constitutes a sin of *irreverence* towards God. This is usurping a right not given to the creature.

That conception is possible even when the sanctioned love union is absent does not deny that God has entrusted procreation to the wedded act, which ought to be a love union sanctioned by consensus.

Here we touch upon a profoundly mysterious area of creation, where what is can either coincide with what ought to be or deviate from it. This is most clearly seen in human freedom: man *can* do what he *ought not* do. He can freely initiate a causal sequence independently of whether he should or should not do so. He can use his freedom in a way opposed to that for which his freedom was granted to him. On the one hand, a causal sequence is not deprived of its efficacy because men abuse it. On the other hand, the fact that this causal sequence *should* serve an end endowed with value is in no way suspended by this abuse. This relation of oughtness remains unchanged and keeps its full validity and reality. Precisely for this reason, every deviation from it is a sin.

When, therefore, someone enters into marriage for, let us say, financial reasons and thereby separates the consensus from its proper context, the marriage is certainly valid; but this does not deny that marriage should be the most intimate union of love, that this union is its meaning, and that God has given it as such to man.

Similarly, the superabundant finality of this union of love remains a relation ordained by God, one which *ought* to exist between the union of love and the generation of a new human being, even though sexual intercourse performed without any love or outside of marriage can lead to conception.

We must endeavor to understand more deeply this mysterious structure of the cosmos: *an infraction of a moral obligation does not in itself cancel the factual order* — that is, the causal efficacy inherent in physical and physiological processes will not be destroyed when we do not act as we ought to; *but neither is the fact that something is morally binding affected by its not being done.*

We must acknowledge this great gift, which God grants to men: He entrusts to man's free will the task of harmonizing things as they are with things as they ought to be. This is man's great dignity and awesome responsibility. In order to divine the meaning of the cosmos in the light of God and understand His message in it, we must take into account how things ought to be and not restrict ourselves to the mere factual order. Therefore, the fact that a man can be generated through sexual intercourse without any love in no way nullifies the mysterious truth that God has entrusted the coming into being of a man to an indissoluble love communion.

## Physiological processes and the creation of human life: is artificial birth control ever a merely "biological" intervention?

Moreover, the conception of a human being, even when it takes place without the prescribed connection with marital love, is not a mere biological fact.

Our entire spiritual and personal life is bound to physiological conditions in various ways, but it is not for this reason a biological reality. Indeed, even baptismal grace or the Real Presence of Christ is attached to an outward sign. In the entire cosmos, then, we repeatedly find this dispensation of divine Providence: realities of a very high order are connected with inferior conditions. But this does not permit us to see only the latter.

The creation of an immortal human person by God through the cooperation of the married couple is therefore in itself never a biological occurrence, though it requires biological conditions. Therefore, the fact that biological laws connect the conjugal act with the creation of a human person does not justify our considering the rupture of the connection only a biological intervention. An extreme case makes this immediately clear: a fatal shot through a man's head is not simply a "biological intervention" but a murder, because a man's life was connected with the physiological processes that were frustrated.

Artificial birth control is thus no mere biological intervention but the severing of a bond which is under the jurisdiction of God alone.

## Biological vs. personal values

In order to justify artificial birth control some people invoke the superiority of personal values over biological values. It is undoubtedly true that personal values rank higher than biological values. But the generation of a new human being, a spiritual person who is an image of God, clearly bears not only a biological value but also an eminently personal value. Whoever is blind to this cannot speak meaningfully of personal values. Again, the fact that the coming into being of a new person is bound by God to the most tender love union is a great mystery which obviously also cannot be regarded as the bearer of a merely biological value. The superabundant finality that binds the becoming of a new human being to the love union in a special way even draws the one who understands it *in conspectu Dei* — before the face of God.

## 6. WHY ARTIFICIAL BIRTH CONTROL IS SINFUL BUT THE RHYTHM METHOD IS NOT

The distinctions we have made above between the two concepts of nature shed new light upon the whole problem of artificial birth control. Above all, we are now in a position to see more clearly the decisive difference between rhythm and artificial birth control. We can now meet more decisively the objection: "Is it not also irreverent to have the explicit intention of avoiding the conception of a new human being without totally abstaining from the conjugal act?"

In the first place the value and meaning of the conjugal act is not affected by the married couple's certainty that it cannot lead to conception. Having seen that this act in its very meaning is a unique expression of spousal love and a mutual donation of self, grounded in consensus, we now understand more clearly that this act is not only allowed, but is possessed of a high value even when conception is not possible. This meaning and value is explicitly recognized in the addresses of Pius XII, in the Council decree *Gaudium et Spes,* as well as in the encyclical *Humanae Vitae.*

In the second place it is definitely allowed *expressly* to avoid conception when the conjugal act takes place *only* in the *God-given* infertile time — that is, only by means of the rhythm method and for legitimate reasons. One would have to be blind to the meaning and value of the conjugal act to say that complete abstinence is morally required when conception is to be avoided for legitimate reasons.

It is clear, therefore, that in the intention itself of avoiding another child for serious reasons there is not the least trace of irreverence toward the mysterious fact that God has entrusted the birth of a person to the spousal love union. We see that only during relatively brief intervals has God Himself linked the conjugal act to the creation of a man. Hence the bond, the active tearing apart of which is a sin, is realized only for a short time in the order of things ordained by God Himself. This also has a meaning. The fact that conception is restricted to a short time implies a word of God. It not only confirms that the bodily union of the spouses has a meaning and value in itself, apart from procreation, but it also leaves open the possibility of avoiding conception if this is desirable for serious reasons. The sin consists in this alone: the sundering by man of what God has joined together — the *artificial, active* severing of the mystery of bodily union from the creative act to which it is bound at the time. Only in this artificial intervention, where one *acts against* the mystery of superabundant finality, is there the sin of irreverence — that is to say, the sin of presumptuously exceeding the creatural rights of man.

Analogously, I may very well wish (and pray) that an incurably sick and extremely suffering man would die. I may abstain from artificially prolonging his life for a matter of hours or days. But I am not allowed to kill him! There is an abyss between desiring someone's death and euthanasia. In both cases the *intention* is the same: out of sympathy I desire that he be delivered from suffering. But in the one case I do nothing that might prolong his suffering, whereas in the other I actively intervene and arrogate to myself a right over life and death that belongs to God alone.

Only when we see the *divinely ordained limits to our active intervention*, the limits that define what is allowed and that play a great role in the whole moral sphere, can we perceive the abyss separating the rhythm method from the use of all kinds of contraceptive devices.[14]

It is therefore desirable that science discover improved methods for ascertaining the infertile days. Pope Pius XII said that he prayed for this, and so should all Christians. Paul VI expresses this wish in *Humanae Vitae*, 24.

As soon as we see the abyss separating the use of rhythm from artificial birth control, we have answered the question: why should artificial birth control be a sin if the use of rhythm is allowed? And

---

14. This distinction between *active intervention* on our part and *letting things* take their course is also drawn in another situation: though no Catholic spouse is allowed to use contraceptive means, he is still not allowed to refuse the marital act even when his partner employs contraceptive means. Here also the distinction between the active and passive attitude is morally decisive.

as soon as we see clearly the sinfulness of artificial birth control, we can and must repudiate the suggestion that it is the proper means of averting dangers that menace marital happiness or averting over-population. No evil in the world, however great, may be avoided through a sinful means. To commit a sin in order to avoid an evil would be to adhere to the ignominious principle: the end justifies the means.

# Part III

# FURTHER OBJECTIONS TO
# THE ENCYCLICAL "HUMANAE VITAE"

# 1. IS THE CHURCH'S TEACHING ON MARRIAGE AND PROCREATION IMPOSSIBLE TO LIVE UP TO?

It is frequently argued that abstaining from the conjugal act during the fertile days of the wife is too great a sacrifice. Some say that the calculation of days destroys the spontaneity of the conjugal act and harms love. Others maintain that the desire of the wife for marital intercourse is strongest just when conception is possible. These objections testify to a merely biological conception of man and the marital act.

No believer can dispute that the readiness for sacrifice belongs to the life of true Christians; this includes not only the resigned acceptance of those trials we cannot avoid, which are beyond our freedom, but also the readiness to accept joyfully all the sacrifices that could be avoided only by committing something morally wrong. (We are even morally obliged to accept death when it can only be avoided by a sin.) He who does not understand this is no Christian.

Moreover, the mutual sacrifice of abstinence is the very antithesis of any impairment of love. The reverence for and obedience to the divine law, which both spouses share, strengthen unity in an exceptional way. Their experiencing of this sacrifice in common can result also in a special actualization of their love. At the same time temporary abstinence is a psychological aid against the spiritually dulling power of habit. Such a sacrifice helps the married couple avoid the danger of treating the conjugal act merely as a means of sexual satisfaction; the sacrifice offered by both the spouses makes them more consciously receptive to the great gift of the conjugal act and more capable of seeing it properly as the fruition of a loving union. We are obviously speaking here of married couples who are called to make this sacrifice for a few days, not of those unusual cases that call for almost total abstinence, which of course means a great sacrifice.

Furthermore, the difficulty of periodic abstinence is often greatly exaggerated: how many people, for example, are ready to undertake temporary abstinence for professional reasons, such as prolonged journeys. I would not like to ask how many couples would be willing to abstain temporarily if they were offered a sum of money for every day of abstinence.

## 2. INHIBITION OF SPONTANEITY

Some assert that the rhythm method frustrates the spontaneity of the marital act. If by spontaneity one means the impulsiveness of mere instincts, this assertion may be true. But such instinctual "spontaneity" is not a characteristic of the right approach to this great love union. We have repeated time and again that the right attitude implies reverence and actualization of the deep love and desire for a real personal union. But if spontaneity means the opposite of a neutral, cool, pragmatic attitude or of forcing ourselves by an effort of will to accomplish something, then obviously spontaneity is an essential requirement for being attracted by the beloved and for a mutual loving concentration on each other.

However, why should this spontaneity be inhibited by ascertaining that the fertile days are over? First, the calendar calculation and the taking of temperature does not immediately precede the union. Secondly, and more important, it would be a symptom of a poor love and of a weak sensuality, if the avoidance of all preliminary planning, or of any practical consideration, were necessary for true spontaneity. It is a feature of our human life that many situations that call for recollection and the absence of pragmatic tensions require preliminary practical considerations. Before traveling to a beautiful country our attention must turn toward many practical, neutral things. Before listening to some sublime music we have to plan and get tickets to the concert. But this tribute paid our earthly condition, as well as other exertions that the fruition of great things require, should not only be joyfully accepted, but also they are illumined by the splendor of the goal they serve. And thus he who is aware of the great gift of this fulfillment of the union with the beloved will not be inhibited in his true spontaneity.

Moreover, this objection discloses a misunderstanding of the role the conjugal act should play in marriage. The union desired in wedded love can and should find many expressions — from holding each other's hand, to the kiss on the lips, and the tender embrace. The conjugal act represents the climax of this union. The degree to which the actualization of this love union, this interpenetration of love, takes place in these expressions depends on the spiritual wakefulness of the lovers, the depth of their love, and on many other physical, mental, and spiritual conditions. A kiss may represent a deeper spiritual union than a conjugal act that is performed without deep awareness or not completely transformed by mutual love. But of course it should not be denied that the conjugal act represents as such an incomparable union in the "becoming one flesh." Here the donation of self is *objectively* something totally new and incomparable, a "disclosure of one's own secret," as I have described it in *In Defense of Purity*.

But it is indeed deplorable when mutual wedded love is not expressed in many noble and tender displays of affection, when the manifestation of wedded love and of the longing for union is restricted to the conjugal act. Such an attitude makes us suspect that this act is desired less as a mutual gift of love than as the satisfaction of isolated sexual drives. Abstention from the conjugal act during the fertile period does not at all oblige married couples to abstain from other ways of expressing their love. The temporary abstention from sexual intercourse will rather help the spouses experience and understand the primacy of the spiritual union in marriage and in the marital act, itself; it will help them see that true happiness can flow only out of the union of love, which receives its highest expression in the marital act.

# Part IV

# THE ENCYCLICAL "HUMANAE VITAE" AND OUR ATTITUDE

# 1. DOES OBEDIENCE PRESUPPOSE INFALLIBILITY?

We often hear today that an encyclical is not infallible. To this we must say first of all that the gift of infallibility is not restricted to *ex cathedra* statements and to dogmas explicitly so defined, but extends also to the official teaching of the Church in all important questions of faith and morals (cf. *Lumen Gentium,* 25). But the proscription of artificial birth control has been solemnly proclaimed by the last popes and repeated by the Second Vatican Council (*Gaudium et Spes,* 51); it represents the unbroken tradition of the magisterium; and thus it is the official teaching of the Church.

But above all, *Lumen Gentium* (25) lays down clearly that every Catholic is also obliged to accept with "inner and outer obedience" the moral law interpreted and proclaimed by the *authentic* though not *ex cathedra* magisterium. Therefore, every Catholic is bound to accept the encyclical *Humanae Vitae* independently of the question of its infallibility, since it is an expression of the authentic magisterium of the Church.

In view of this it is nonsense to say that the encyclical is only the private opinion of the Pope to which one could oppose the positions of individual theologians and even laymen as equally tenable opinions. Those who say this and who exhort the Pope to "take back" the teaching of the Church on artificial birth control reveal an ignorance of the nature of the Church and betray a loss of that faith which alone entitles someone to call himself a Catholic.

## 2. NATURAL MORAL LAW AND THE MAGISTERIUM

One often hears the objection that though the Church is competent to interpret the moral law revealed in the Bible, it is not competent to interpret the natural moral law. This objection completely misunderstands the relation between natural and supernatural moral law. In *The Trojan Horse in the City of God* (Ch. VI and VII), I have shown that Christian revelation necessarily presupposes certain basic natural truths. Therefore, all relativism, determinism, subjectivism, naturalism, and immanentism are completely incompatible with Christian revelation.

One of the essential tasks of the magisterium of the Church is to protect against the errors of the age the basic truths which are implicit in and presupposed by Christian faith. For this reason, it is also the duty of the Church to interpret the true natural moral law, which the supernatural morality revealed in the Gospels presupposes. Therefore, the objection that the encyclical goes beyond an exposition of the revealed moral law and has no Biblical basis is in any case beside the point.

## 3. SACRIFICE AND THE ABSOLUTE PRIMACY OF THE MORAL SPHERE

Though a great sacrifice be demanded of those married couples who cannot determine the fecund days with certainty, we nevertheless know that *no sacrifice* will detain the true Christian from obeying God's holy law. We may and should pray that science will render the rhythm method absolutely certain, and thereby lift a heavy cross from certain married couples. But once again we wish to repeat that every true Christian is conscious of the deep and rudimentary meaning of sacrifice in this earthly life. The consciousness of our creaturehood, the understanding that we should receive gratefully from God's hand all gifts of happiness, but also that we should accept willingly the crosses He imposes on us — all this is fundamental to the Christian attitude. And inseparable from the Christian faith is the recognition of the absolute primacy of obeying God and His holy law, rather than indulging our wishes, as well as the knowledge that our earthly existence is a pilgrimage and that this earth is a *vallis lacrimarum,* a valley of tears. Only in the light of Christ's words, "He who would be my disciple, let him take up his cross and follow me," can we give the proper God-willed response to all the crosses and sacrifices in our life. And among these crosses are the sacrifices that a Christian marriage can impose on us. The question of birth control can be properly understood and judged only in this light. Any man who believes he has the right to procure whatever he deems necessary for his happiness, without concerning himself with the holy laws of God, places himself outside of the Christian orbit.

# Part V

# CONSCIENCE AND THE MAGISTERIUM

## 1. CONSCIENCE AND THE KNOWLEDGE OF THE MORAL LAW

The thesis that the decision to practice contraception ought to be left to the consciences of individual Catholics has become quite fashionable. It implies, however, a confusion — an utterly false understanding of conscience. Conscience does not instruct us about whether something is morally good or evil; rather, this question must be answered *before* conscience can speak. We use a spiritual organ completely different from conscience when we comprehend moral values and disvalues. It is not through conscience that we understand that murder is evil, or that theft is morally wrong, or that justice is good, etc. In all these cases either we are taught by a faculty for grasping moral values and disvalues, the faculty of value perception, or we are informed by a moral authority. The difference between conscience and the perception of moral values becomes clearer if we consider that upon seeing some other person act unjustly, or upon being deeply moved by the goodness and purity of a man, it is not conscience that discloses to us the value and disvalue in question.

Conscience speaks only when our own action or

omission is at issue. Its primary function is to warn us in concrete situations *not* to do certain things that we know are morally wrong: it mainly admonishes us to avoid a moral evil. It also urges us to do good when failure to do so would be a sin.

Conscience is the *advocatus Dei,* God's advocate, in the soul of man: it warns us when we are tempted to do something wrong or when someone tries to persuade us to consent to something morally wrong. Conscience is the mysterious voice that makes us aware of the fearful and unique seriousness of the moral question: when evil desire or weak compliance rises up, it confronts us with the full majesty of the imperious summons not to offend God by an immoral deed. But conscience always presupposes a knowledge of the real or alleged moral character of a contemplated action.

To summarize: first, examination of conscience about things past and the consideration in conscience of some future deed refer only to one's own behavior; secondly, conscience refers to a particular, concrete case; third, its primary function is to warn us not to do certain things — it is mainly concerned with the *avoidance* of immoral actions or the condemnation of past actions — though it also urges us to do good when failure to do so would be a sin. But conscience *always presupposes* a moral conviction, which does not originate in conscience but either in a capacity for perceiving moral values and disvalues or in accepting instruction from a moral authority.

But we must not forget that man's ability to grasp moral values is weakened by many factors. There are many forms of moral value-blindness. The words of the psalmist, *"Omnis homo mendax"* (Every man is a liar), are particularly relevant in this context.

## 2. CONSCIENCE AND DESIRE

It is important to realize that conscience raises its voice only in the name of what we understand to be our moral duty and not in the name of our wishes and inclinations. If I am tempted to do something that seems pleasurable, it is not my conscience that urges me to yield. It raises its voice only in the name of morality, warning me not to give in to desires I know to be evil.

To be sure, when my moral convictions are wrong, conscience will warn me to abstain from something that is in reality morally unobjectionable or it may advise me to do something morally wrong. With sorrowful heart the Corsican Matteo Falconi (in Mérimée's novel) shoots his only son because his conscience — misinformed by a false moral conviction (in this case concerning family honor) — tells him that he is morally obliged to do so. Nevertheless, his misinformed conscience speaks in the name of morality and not in the name of his wishes and desires.

If a doctor were to say to someone: "It is your duty to your wife to give up smoking because you will kill yourself and leave your wife a widow if you continue"; and if he were then to answer: "My conscience forbids me to stop smoking," the absurdity would be immediately apparent. Contrast this with the following statement: "My conscience tells me that I should give up smoking, despite the great effort it will cost me." It becomes clear to us how impossible it is to make conscience the advocate of what we like instead of what we morally should do. Yet, attempts to pass off our desires as the urgings of conscience are quite fashionable. Newman spoke of this masquerade as follows:

> When men advocate the rights of conscience, they in no sense mean the rights of the Creator, nor the duty to Him, in thought and deed, of the creature; but the right of thinking, speaking, writing, and acting, according to their judgment or their humour, without any thought of God at all . . . . Conscience has rights because it has duties: but in this age, with a large portion of the public, it is the very right and freedom of conscience to dispense with conscience, to ignore a Lawgiver and Judge, to be independent of unseen obligations . . . . Conscience is a stern monitor, but in this century it has been superseded by a counterfeit, which the eighteen centuries prior to it never heard of, and could not have mistaken for it, if they had. It is the right of self-will.[15]

Analogously, it is spurious to say that the question of whether or not a couple submits to the papal prohibition of artificial birth control should be decided by their conscience. Those who put forth such arguments obviously cannot assume that the use of the rhythm method instead of the pill is immoral and that thus their conscience forbids them to practice it. The conflict here is not one between two duties but between something which makes their life easier and allows them the unhindered enjoyment of married life on the one hand, and on the other committing a moral wrong, namely using arti-

---

15. *Difficulties of Anglicans,* II (London: Longmans, 1914), 250.

ficial contraceptives. It would only make sense if they would say: "We do not see why the use of the pill should be morally wrong, our conscience does not warn us against it." But this would show ignorance of man's inclination to self-deception and of his becoming the victim of moral value-blindness. It further betrays incredible pride in that they believe themselves to be more competent in moral questions than the Church — a position which for a Catholic means that he no longer fully believes in the teaching authority of the Church. It is a false assertion to say that there is a conflict between a precept and the individual's conscience when his conscience fails to warn him to desist from what attracts him. A conflict with one's conscience can arise only when something is imposed on one which one considers morally evil. Nobody can honestly say: "My conscience forbids my temporary abstinence in marriage." This would be to mistake two possible situations: on the one hand, the tragic situation in which a legitimate authority might impose on me an action which I consider to be morally evil, and thus my conscience would raise its voice and warn me not to obey; on the other hand, a situation in which a legitimate authority forbids an action as immoral, and I cannot see *why* it is immoral; here my conscience can never speak its solemn "No" against the commandment of this legitimate authority, but can only remain silent, while I yield to my wishes and desires.

Some have argued that in the question of artificial birth control the alternative is between two evils. They say that it is not true that here there is only a conflict between our wishes and a moral commandment, but rather that there is a conflict between the evil of artificial contraception and the evil of endangering marriage — a good with a high value which God commands us to respect and protect. In these cases they say, the married couple can and should choose the lesser of the two evils, according to their consciences. This argument is wrong for several reasons.

First, the thesis that the use of rhythm may harm a happy marriage is more than doubtful — as I have shown above when dealing with the question of whether or not the observance of rhythm and avoidance of contraceptives require too great a sacrifice. Secondly, it equates a moral evil, the use of artificial contraception, with a misfortune, a morally relevant evil — the harming of marriage. And here all the amoralism of situation ethics appears, which showed its ugly face in the "majority report" of the papal commission on birth control.[16] We must say here with greatest emphasis that we are never allowed to do something morally evil in order to prevent a misfortune. Sins, which offend God, and great misfortunes (the destruction of high values through no moral fault of ours) are absolutely incomparable. Sin alone offends God; no misfortune — however great — is commensurate with the fearful disharmony issuing from an offense of God. This is so, not only because God is infinitely more important than man, but also because for man himself sin is the greatest evil: sin has an eternal resonance, whereas all other

---

16.  Cf. The thesis of the "majority report" as quoted by His Excellency Bishop Höffner, Bishop of Münster, Germany, in the *Wanderer,* 17 Oct. 1968.

evils are restricted to the temporal order. The pagan, Socrates, said: "It is better for man to suffer injustice than to commit it" (*Gorgias*).

It is extremely important to distinguish between moral values (such as purity, kindness, justice) and morally *relevant* values (such as the value of man's life, his happiness, his right of property, etc.). These latter values are morally relevant because to respect them is morally good, to disrespect them, morally evil. But respect for them is itself the bearer of a *moral* value. In the free response of man to these goods a new type of value — the moral value — is born. In disrespecting these goods a moral disvalue comes into existence.

It is certainly true that when we have to decide between two morally relevant goods which exclude each other, we should *ceteris paribus* choose the higher one. For instance, we have to neglect a promise when a great emergency calls for our intervention. In such a case two morally relevant values are in conflict and not a moral value on the one hand and a morally relevant value on the other; also there are not two actions in conflict, but an omission on the one hand and an active deed on the other.

There is a decisive difference between giving preference to the call of a higher value in my action, by omitting the call of the lower, and destroying the lower good through my own *active* intervention. In an emergency we are even morally obliged to help the one who needs it more, whose rescue is more important. By doing so we may be forced with a bleeding heart to omit helping another person who also is in danger. But there obviously lies an abyss between this case and the one in which I would kill that innocent person in order to save a more important one or in order to save a greater number of persons. In the first case I save the one whose life I consider a higher good without doing anything against the other. In the second I kill an innocent person and thereby commit a sin. I offend God in order to save the one whose life I consider a higher good. In the first case two morally relevant values are at stake and I choose the higher. In the second case a moral wrong (disvalue) is realized by my intervention in order to save a morally relevant good. This is again the hideous principle: The end justifies the means. It considers the protection of a good endowed with high values more important than offending God.

This conclusion has been heard often. It betrays a strikingly primitive contradiction. It is a fiction to say that a couple wanting to follow the command of the Church but still conscious of their duty to preserve the stability and harmony of their marriage are forced to choose between two duties. Couples who are faithful children of the Church and eager to fulfill God's will could never consider the possibility of adultery as inevitable if they had to make the sacrifice of using rhythm in their marital life. It is a form of blackmail of God to say: Either I give free reign to my desires or I will fall into sin. This is an attitude which is out of the question even for a Catholic of little faith. The very basis of Christianity is the awareness that our situation on earth due to the fall of man implies a fight against our desires in order to obey God's commandments and reach eternal beatitude. Never are we entitled to say: If I abstain from committing one sin, I will inevitably commit another.

> . . . Who is such a fool as to say, let us sin now,
> that we may obviate a possible future sin; let us now
> commit murder, lest we perhaps afterwards should
> commit adultery?[17]

The endangering of marriage by partial abstinence is never an inevitable process. Free will can always intervene and can resist any alleged impairment to the stability and unity of marriage. The necessity of choosing between these two evils thus cannot occur here. A married couple of moral elevation, who treasured the stability and harmony of their marriage and understood the deep value of their love union, could never assume that injury to their mutual love — and even committing adultery — were matters beyond their control, that is, beyond their free-will. It is reckless and unreasonable to suppose that they could consider it as an inevitable consequence of their obeying the Church's teaching. Rather they would turn to prayer and be full of hope that with the grace of God they will be able by their free will to resist all temptations.

In this contrived problem of a choice between two evils, one can see a confusion between asceticism and moral commandments. If severe fasting or the reduction of sleep as a voluntary ascetic practice had the effect of making a person nervous and irritable and therefore a burden to his family, it is obvious that he should refrain from his ascetic practices. In this case, because the consequences result

---

17. St. Augustine, *The City of God,* I, 25.

from physiological causes, they have something of an automatic character; moreover, in refraining from ascetic practices he neither neglects a duty nor commits a sin. In this case, indeed, it is his duty to omit something which, though certainly good, is not a moral obligation, and the evil consequences are to a great extent not dependent on his free will. But there is a decisive difference between ascetic practices and moral commandments. Man is never allowed to violate a moral commandment, that is, actually to sin, in order to avoid possible though not inevitable bad consequences, even possible future sins.

It is also very naive to assume that when faced with two conflicting real duties, one requiring a sacrifice and the other coinciding with his personal inclinations, a person will as a matter of course be able to decide objectively. We have seen that the use of rhythm does not in reality mean a conflict of two duties. But also, the couple who has the moral awareness and true religious desire to conform to God's will will distrust their own decisions when one of the duties coincides with their wishes and inclinations. Even a pagan of high moral standard would assume that some morally trustworthy person whose personal wishes are not involved would be able to advise him more objectively as to his real duty. But if this is true for all those having enough moral honesty and a minimum of knowledge of man's propensity for self-deception, how much more will the Christian see that he needs help in order to see clearly and objectively what is the right thing to do. A Catholic will turn to his spiritual director or confessor for help in order to be sure not to be fooled by his desires.

## 3. COMPETENCE AND THE MAGISTERIUM

We must now consider the curious but widespread notion that persons "competent" in this matter may come to a different conclusion from the one the Church has always had and has recently reaffirmed in *Humanae Vitae*. Before discussing the validity of this thesis, the meaning of the word "competence" must be briefly analyzed. First, there is the competence of practical authority, which refers not only to its authenticity and legitimacy but also to its extent or range. Apart from the authority of God Himself, all true authority is restricted to a certain realm. The President of the United States has the competence to declare war in co-operation with Congress, but he definitely has not got the competence to tell me whom to marry, or to tell a musician whether he should compose symphonies or chamber music. The essence of totalitarianism lies in the arrogation of limitless competence in all realms of human existence, and in the case of a totalitarian state it manifests itself in infringing on the most intimate realms of the individual's life, on his *human* rights.

Even the incomparably higher and holy authority of the Church and of the Pope as Vicar of Christ, does not extend to everything. At the moment we are not yet concerned with the Church's theoretical, absolute authority in matters of faith and morals, but with her practical authority to prohibit and to command something. Though this authority — in contradistinction to any worldly authority — does reach into the most intimate sphere of the person, it is nevertheless restricted. It does not extend to such questions as what profession a person should choose, whom he should marry or not marry, except in those cases where canonical obstacles stand in the way.

"Competence" can also mean something quite different: it can refer to the capacity to judge certain matters, to the qualities which give weight to judgment. In faith and morals there is for the Catholic just one absolutely competent authority — the Church. Only the Church through her authentic magisterium is competent to decide what is in accordance with Christian revelation or what is a sin. This competence is absolute because the Holy Spirit guides the Church. But all merely human competence is only relative.

This relative competence varies to a great extent according to the matter in question. For example, we assume more or less that a mechanic in a repair shop is competent to repair our car. But he may prove to be incompetent. When we go to a doctor for a check-up, we assume he is competent in his field — for he has passed examinations and received a license to practice medicine. His reputation may give us additional reason to believe him competent. Though his competence remains a relative competence, it entitles him to make judgments in his field and makes it reasonable for us to accept his advice. We can speak in the same way of the competence of a pharmacist, a physicist, a lawyer, or an historian. In all such cases, competence is established by examinations, diplomas, success, reputation, and the like. But when it comes to philosophical or artistic fields there is no analogous basis for determining competence. That a "philosopher" has passed his examinations brilliantly and is famous does not prove anything about his real competence. As in the case of a musician or artist, his competence depends exclusively on his depth and giftedness. Philosophical or artistic competence may coincide with great success, influence and fame, but need not. There have been great artists and philosophers whose genius was not recognized in their lifetime but only much later; in any case competence here is not guaranteed by any diploma or reputation. And it, too, remains relative.

In moral questions a relative competence can be attributed to a person of high moral standards and intelligence. We are justified in asking the advice of a person who is reliable, deep, conscientious, and rooted in his Christian faith. We would never ask him whether or not a given action was sinful if the Church had already answered the question and we already knew her answer. We would, however, seek his advice about particular decisions, about what we should give preference to in a concrete case; for example, we might ask which of two people it is our greater duty to help (if it is impossible to help both). We rightly believe that his opinion may be more objective than our own, and we can say of such a friend that we consider him competent to judge about this concrete situation. If a person has a spiritual director he deeply admires, whose deep faith, loyalty to the teaching of the Church, and spiritual wisdom he has experienced, he will consider him competent to judge a concrete moral problem.

Now, it is competence in this second meaning of the term that is at issue in the discussion about the encyclical *Humanae Vitae*. It is asserted that "competent'' persons are entitled to form their own judgment about artificial contraception and are thus not strictly bound to accept the teaching of the Church as proclaimed by the Pope. Is it asserted of these "competent" persons that they are "experts" in love? in marital happiness? in the psychological consequences of the use of rhythm? Or are they experts in morality? Have they so keen a sense of moral good and evil that their moral standards are uncommonly high, and that they lead saintly lives? If "competence" here refers to the nature of love, marital happiness, and the effect of the use of rhythm, then we can say that it is in no way guaranteed by the fact that a person has studied many statistics, read many books about marriage, and feels himself to be an expert. The fact that he has studied this problem and read many books (which books?) on this topic is not the slightest proof that he has a profound understanding of the nature of love, marriage, marital happiness, and all the factors which may play a role in temporary abstinence and the use of rhythm. Notwithstanding all his studies, he may be absolutely blind to the nature of marriage. Only a true understanding of spousal love, only spiritual depth and true contact with reality, only the capacity for grasping things in their real nature, can give him some competence to answer questions in this field.

Before we enter into a discussion of whether or not such a relative competence can ever entitle anyone to neglect a papal prohibition, let us note that here no standard has been established for determining whether a person has the required competence. It has been left for the person himself to decide his own competence. But we cannot expect everyone to pass a valid judgment about his own qualifications. For example, we cannot expect everyone to be able to judge whether he is intelligent or not. It is well known that there is a certain type of stupidity which precisely consists in believing oneself to be particularly intelligent even though it is far from being the case. The same applies to questions such as: Are you mature? It is a special sign of immaturity, typical of puberty, to be convinced of one's own maturity.

Thus, the statement that if someone judges himself to be competent he need not submit to the Church's prohibition is doomed from the start, because it is left up to the person to decide for himself whether or not he is competent. It should thus be clear to every reasonable person that to grant the spouses the capacity to pass judgment on their own competence in a moral question like artificial birth control betrays a ludicrous naiveté.

Are priests and moral theologians perhaps the only competent ones? Is a priest in the confessional entitled to disavow the encyclical if he believes he is one of the competent people? May he advise the faithful according to his own opinion? But, as we have indicated, it is equally naive to leave it to the individual priest to decide whether or not he is competent. Has the priest perhaps by his ordination been liberated from the dangers of pride and self-deception? Is he capable of deciding objectively whether or not he is intelligent, mature, and competent in questions of morality? Certainly, unlike the layman, he shares in the authority of the Church, but only as long as he faithfully supports the official teaching of the Church. As soon as his own ideas diverge from the official teaching of the Church, he loses all official authority to advise the faithful and places himself on the level of a layman.

Moreover, we must emphasize that the very idea that competence could entitle anyone to defy the prohibition of artificial birth control, or even to preach the contrary, implies a complete denial of the Church's teaching authority. The only question that matters in this context is: Is artificial contraception a sin or is it not a sin? The Pope, in a long-awaited and dramatically important pronouncement, in accordance with the unbroken traditional teaching of the Church, says: Yes, it is a sin. If anyone assumes that the Pope is wrong and that he knows better he is clearly disavowing his belief in the teaching authority of the Church in morals and thereby ceases to be an authentic Catholic.

But to say, as some have said, that the papal teaching is right but only binding for the "incompetent" is self-contradictory and a plain inanity. If artificial birth control is a sin, then no Catholic can consider himself exempt from obeying — and thus entitled to sin — because of his alleged competence.

Implied in this dispensation of the competent ones is the idea that the teaching authority of the Church in morals is binding on the simple-minded, "incompetent" people — the *hoi polloi* — but not on the superior, competent man who can judge for himself. This conviction represents a superstitious idolization of science, of expertise, of ideological speculation, which actually would divide mankind into two classes, the one required to obey God's commandments and the other not: the incompetent and the competent. This would indeed be so esoteric as to be Gnosticism, pure and simple. When we analyze the meaning of competence in this context, instead of inadvertently swallowing the slogan, we are compelled to note that it conceals a grave error. This division of the faithful into the competent and the incompetent, imperils a more fundamental part of the Christian faith than the Church's teaching on birth control. It either leads to a denial of the magisterium of the Church in morals or it, in effect, places some persons, the competent ones (why not rather say Nietzsche's Superman?), above morality. We saw how impossible it is for conscience to tell a Catholic he may practice artificial birth control. Introducing the new notion of competence only compounds the error of this thesis of situation ethics.

Thus it seems that the introduction of the idea of competence into the discussion of *Humanae Vitae* is rather an attempt to avoid both a direct contradiction of the papal prohibition (with all the inevitable consequences of open disloyalty) and a conflict with the dissidents in the Church. One thus manages to appear at once loyal to the Pope without losing one's popularity among the "progressives." St. Augustine says:

> Who is the hireling who, seeing the approach of the wolf, takes flight? He who seeks himself and does not seek what is of Jesus Christ: he who does not dare to frankly admonish the sinner (1 Tim. 5, 20). See, someone has sinned, gravely sinned, he should be admonished, excluded from the Church. But excluded from the Church he will become its enemy and will try to ensnare it and harm it where he can. Now [the hireling], the one who seeks himself and not what is of Jesus Christ will be silent and not give any admonition, in order not to lose what he seeks, namely, the advantages of personal friendship, and in order to avoid the unpleas-

antness (the worry) or personal enmity. The wolf
at that moment takes hold of the sheep to throttle
them . . . . You are silent, O hireling, and do not
admonish . . . . Your silence was your flight. You
are silent, you were afraid. Fear is the flight of the
soul.[18]

## 4. THE INTERPRETATION OF THE OBJECTIVE MORAL LAW BY THE MAGISTERIUM OF THE CHURCH AND THE DUTY OF THE INDIVIDUAL CONSCIENCE

Given man's propensity to moral value-blindness,
as we saw before, it should be clear that whoever
regards his subjective ideas of what is morally allowed as the last word is the victim of great self-
deception. Every believing Catholic, however, is
convinced that the moral teaching that derives from
Revelation, as well as that which derives from the
natural moral law, and which the magisterium of
the Church authentically interprets and applies to
specific problems, takes unhesitating precedence over
his subjective opinions about moral questions. But to
assert that the individual conscience ought to decide
whether artificial birth control is morally allowable
is moreover inane, for this is to demand of conscience what it can never perform, as we have seen.

In reality, to leave the moral decision up to the
individual amounts to saying: The Church does not
know what is morally good and evil; the individual
alone can decide this — a position which denies
both Revelation as well as the magisterium, and in

---

18. St. Augustine, *Tractatus in Joannem*, XLVI, 7-8,
in *Patrologia Latina*, XXXV, 1731-1732.

the final analysis dissolves all objectively valid morality and leads to total amoralism.

But what has been said does not detract from the fact that conscience has an all important role to play in man's moral life. The individual conscience must *co-operate* in all moral questions; it has the duty of warning us against acting unkindly or dishonestly, just as much as warning us against the sin of artificial birth control. To conscience is always committed an enormously important task: to remind us of and make present to us the awesome seriousness of all moral commands in concrete situations, to summon us to moral vigilance and honesty, and to protect us from self-deception.

The antithesis of conscience is unscrupulousness. The man who is indifferent to the question of whether something is good or bad, sinful or licit, is unscrupulous. The man who is blind to the ultimate gravity of the moral order, to the offense against God constituted by sin, is unscrupulous. He also is unscrupulous who deliberately silences the voice of his conscience and frivolously, without bothering about whether something is good or bad, abandons himself to his impulses. Also, he who is not conscious of man's capacity for self-deception and possibility of being value-blind is unscrupulous and acts irresponsibly. But the true co-operation of conscience, whose voice admonishes us to full responsibility, presupposes a knowledge of what is fundamentally good or evil, pleasing to God or sinful, allowed or not allowed. And in the case of a Catholic, only he who humbly and gratefully accepts the moral law revealed by God and the definition of what is morally good or not good as explicitly proclaimed by the Church is truly conscientious and truly responsible. The voice of the Holy Church, however, *does not replace conscience,* does not stifle it or call upon us to renounce responsibility, but rather offers conscience the indispensable information about what is good or evil. It protects and supports our conscience against all the tendencies of our fallen nature that try to drown out its voice.

# Part VI

# THE ENCYCLICAL "HUMANAE VITAE" AND THE CREDO OF PAUL VI

We should evaluate the depth and sublimity of the encyclical *Humanae Vitae* in the light of the considerations given above and accept it not only reverently in obedience to the representative of Christ on earth, but also with grateful joy. For here — in contrast to the one-sided emphasis on procreation that marked many previous treatments of the subject — the full meaning of the conjugal act as a union of love and a mutual self-donation is duly acknowledged. This does not in the least constitute any contradiction to the earlier teaching of the Church, but is rather an organic development: what was already alluded to in the Council of Trent (Denzinger 1797-99), what Pius XII so marvelously expressed in several allocutions, what the Pastoral Constitution *Gaudium et Spes* (48-51) clearly stated, has been explicitly included here by way of completing and perfecting the teaching on marriage. Hand in hand with this enriched conception of marriage, the grounds for the sinfulness of artificial birth control are convincingly given: the irreverent intervention in the mystery of the bond between the most sublime union of love and the generation of a person, man's transgression, his going beyond his role as servant of God to usurp a right which belongs to God alone. And the abyss that separates active, artificial intervention from the observance of rhythm is clearly presented in the encyclical.

We must above all realize that the encyclical *Humanae Vitae* can be understood only in the light of the glorious *Credo* of the Holy Father. It is no accident that shortly before *Humanae Vitae,* at the close of the year of faith, the Holy Father solemnly recalled the fundamental truths of Christian Revelation. The belief in these constitutes the decisive criterion of whether a person can still honestly call himself a Catholic.

In the position taken toward the *Credo* we stand at the crossroads where men ultimately part company. It draws the line for the discernment of spirits. The understanding of the fact that artificial birth control is an abandonment of *religio,* of the reverent submission to God, an exceeding of the limits of our creaturehood, a contradiction of our reverent dwelling before God, presupposes that one is not infected by anthropocentrism, by secularization, and "progressivism." Therefore, anything said by theologians, priests, or laymen who no longer unequivocally stand upon the ground of the *Credo* proclaimed by the Pope can carry no weight for the faithful Catholic.

Every true Catholic must rejoice also when he is allowed to see clearly that the Church does not conform to the "majority opinion" but to the Word of God and that the Holy Father must proclaim the truth even when it goes against the current of the times. The supernatural character of the Holy Church reveals itself in a blissful way in that she, in contrast to all merely human institutions, speaks *opportune-importune,* in season and out of season.

The encyclical *Humanae Vitae*, in which the Holy Father teaches us clearly the true moral nature of artificial birth control, enables the individual to know exactly what God expects of him and appeals to our conscience not to offend God. Every Christian who does not live in an illusion about himself and about the danger of self-deception in moral matters must be grateful — however great the sacrifices he has to accept — to know how he *should* act without offending God. This should matter incomparably more to every Christian than the fulfillment of his personal desires. Christ said, "Seek ye *first* the kingdom of God," and, "One thing is necessary."